THE FUTURE
Bleak OR Bright?

Chicago, Illinois

°© 2006 Raintree
Published by Raintree,
A division of Capston Global Library, LLC.
Chicago, Illinois

Customer Service   888–363–4266

Visit our website at www.raintreelibrary.com

Printed in the United States of America in Eau Claire, Wisconsin. 052013   007416R

Library of Congress Cataloging-in-Publication Data
Spilsbury, Louise.
 The future--bleak or bright? : Earth's resources /
Louise and Richard
Spilsbury.
    p. cm.
 Includes bibliographical references and index.
 ISBN 978-1-4109-1928-1 (library binding)
 ISBN 978-1-4109-1959-5 (pbk.)
 ISBN 1-4109-1928-5 (library binding)
 ISBN 1-4109-1959-5 (pbk.)
 1. Natural resources--Management--Juvenile
literature. 2.
Conservation of natural resources--Juvenile literature.
I. Spilsbury, Richard,
 1963- II. Title.
 HC85.S65 2004
 333.7--dc22
                                        2005009540

The author and publishers are grateful to the following for permission to reproduce copyright material: Corbis pp. 10, 17 (Yann Arthus-Bertrand); Corbis Royalty-Free p. 28b; Ecoscene p. 24-25; Empics p. 8 (EPA); Getty Images pp. 6-7 (Robert Giroux), 9 (Photodisc), 16 (Stone), 26-27 (Stone), 28top (Photodisc), 29b (Photodisc), 29top (Photodisc); Harcourt Education Ltd p. 14-15 thumbnails (Tudor Photography); NaturePL p. 18 (Bernard Castelein); Panos Pictures p. 12-13 (Mark Henley); Photolibrary.com pp. 11 (E.J. West), 14-15 (Paul Redding), 22-23 (Walter Bibikow); Science Photo Library pp. 4-5 (Planetary Visions Ltd), 20-21 (Scott Camazine/K. Visscher).

Cover illustrations by Darren Lingard. Photograph of the Earth from space reproduced with permission of Science Photo Library (Planetary Visions Ltd).

Illustrations by Darren Lingard.

The publishers would like to thank Nancy Harris and Harold Pratt for their assistance in the preparation of this book.

Every effort has been made to contact copyright holders of any material reproduced in this book. Any omissions will be rectified in subsequent printings if notice is given to the publishers.

The paper used to print this book comes from sustainable resources.

Disclaimer

Acknowledgments

Contents

Some words are printed in bold, **like this**. You can find out what they mean on page 30. You can also look in the box at the bottom of the page where they first appear.

Bleak or Bright?

People need **natural resources**.
Natural resources are things we use
from our planet. Water, trees, air,
and **oil** are natural resources.

We need natural resources
to live. The future could be
bleak for all living things
if we run out of natural
resources. But . . .

natural resources	materials that people use that come from Earth, such as water
oil	natural resource found under the ground that people use for fuel

If we use Earth's natural resources carefully, then they will last into the future. In this book, we'll think about how to save our natural resources. Everyone can make a difference and help to make the future bright.

◀ *Will the future of the world be bleak or bright? Will the air be smoky or clean? Will there be forests of trees or bare land? Will rivers be dirty or clear and full of life?*

Blackout!

This city is in darkness. All the lights are off.
Television screens are blank. Rooms are chilly.
There is only cold food to eat.

The city has shut down because the **electricity**
is off. This doesn't happen very often. However,
it could happen much more in the future.

Some people use **natural resources** to make electricity. Gas and coal come from deep underground. They are **nonrenewable resources**. That means there is a limited amount of them. They will run out sooner or later.

Keep the future bright

You can use less electricity and help to save natural resources by:

- ☼ *Turning off lights when you leave a room*
- ☼ *Turning off your TV and computer when you are not using them*
- ☼ *Putting on a sweater instead of turning up the heating.*

electricity   source of power that makes machines work
nonrenewable resources   materials that people use that will run out one day

These cars are waiting to ▲ get fuel at a gas station.

Going Nowhere

Many people use a car even for short journeys. Yet traveling might not be so easy in the future. If people don't stop using so much fuel, it may start to run out. There will then be more lines of cars like the one in the photo.

Cars and other vehicles run on a fuel made from **oil**. Oil is a **fossil fuel**, just as coal and gas are. Fossil fuels formed from the bodies of living things that died millions of years ago. All fossil fuels are **nonrenewable resources**. Oil is running out faster than other nonrenewable resources.

We can save fuel

One way to save fuel is to use cars less often. You could walk or cycle to school. For longer distances, you could take a bus or train or share a ride with friends.

fossil fuel material formed from the remains of plants and animals that died millions of years ago

Endless Supplies

One way to make sure the future is bright is to use more **renewable resources**. These are resources that will never run out. Wind and sunlight are renewable resources. The movement of water is a renewable resource, too. Moving water has **energy**. This means it can make a change happen. This energy can be used to work machines that make **electricity**.

*This car runs on **solar power**. Shiny ▲ panels trap the energy in sunlight and turn it into electricity. This electricity makes the engine work.*

▼ People build wind turbines like these to use the energy of the wind. The wind spins the turbines around. The turbines use the energy from the wind to make electricity.

energy   ability to make things move or change
renewable resources   resources that can be replaced
solar power   electricity made by using light or heat from the Sun

Life on the Streets

Imagine walking down this street. The dirty air makes your eyes sting. It makes you choke and cough. There is so much **pollution** in the air that some people wear masks over their faces. Breathing air like this is bad for you.

Most air pollution happens when people burn **fossil fuels**. Oil, coal, and gas are fossil fuels. They are burned in **power stations** and factories. The smoke from power stations and factories causes air pollution. Cars and airplanes also burn fossil fuels. The fumes from engines cause air pollution.

Be an air freshener!

Factories burn fossil fuels to make things such as computers, cell phones, and sneakers. This causes air pollution. You can help reduce air pollution by buying things second-hand. You can also try to mend things like bikes and skateboards if they break. Rent DVDs instead of buying them.

12

▼ *People can hardly see where they are going when smoke and fumes blow across city streets.*

pollution   something that poisons or damages air, water, or land
power station   place that makes electricity

Not a Load of Garbage!

One way to save **natural resources** is to **recycle** things instead of throwing them away. Recycling means changing waste into something that can be used again. Aluminium cans are an example. Factories use a lot of **electricity** to make metal for new cans. Making recycled cans uses far less electricity. Many of the things we throw away can be used to make other things.

Plastic bottles can be can be turned into fleece jackets.

Worn-out tires can be made into pencil cases.

recycle   change waste into something that can be used again

Old plastic cups can be turned into pencils.

Glass can be melted down and made into new jars and bottles.

Empty cans can be crushed, melted, and made into new cans.

Old clothes can be made into new clothes, blankets, and rugs.

Water World

Water is a precious **natural resource**. You can live for weeks without food. Yet you can only live for a few days without water.

Most of the water on Earth is ocean water. This is too salty for people to use. People need fresh water to survive.

We use water at home for things such as drinking, washing, and flushing toilets. Factories use water to stop machines from getting hot. Farmers spray water on their **crops**. Huge amounts of water are needed every day. In the future, there may be times when there is not enough fresh water for everyone to use.

Saving water

You can reduce the amount of water you use by:

- ♪ *Taking a shower instead of a bath. Showers use much less water.*
- ♪ *Turning off taps completely. A dripping tap can waste 2.2 gallons (10 liters) of water each day.*
- ♪ *Collecting rainwater to water plants and wash cars.*

crops plants that farmers grow to sell

▼ This river is in Australia. Not much rain falls here. Plants can only grow in the wet soil near the river.

17

The fish in this lake ▼ have died because the water was polluted.

Dirty waters

Waste has flowed into this river. The water has become dirty and smelly. There is too much **pollution** for animals and plants to live in it. Many of the fish that live in the water have been killed. There is pollution in the water of many rivers and lakes.

People cannot use polluted water. It can make them sick if they drink it or wash in it. People are working hard to keep water clean for the future. In some countries there are rules to stop factories from dumping waste into rivers.

In some cities the **sewage** from toilets goes straight into rivers. Many cities now clean the water first so that the sewage doesn't pollute rivers.

Help keep water clean

The things you put down your drain may flow into rivers. Grease, cooking oil, and cleaning fluids can pollute the water in the rivers. Try not to pour these things down your drain.

sewage   human waste carried away from people's toilets and drains

Forest on fire!

Some people start fires like this to clear trees in forests. Then they build houses on the land or use it for farming. Many other trees are cut down for wood. People use the wood to make paper, tables, and other things.

Cutting down trees in a forest is called **deforestation**. Deforestation puts living things in danger. Wild plants and animals live in forests. Trees also give out a gas called **oxygen**. We need oxygen in the air we breathe. Without trees we will have less oxygen.

deforestation	when trees in a forest are cut down
oxygen	gas in the air that we need to breathe
sustainable	something that keeps going and does not run out

Tree tales

In a **sustainable** forest, people plant new trees to replace any that are cut down. Buying wood that comes from a sustainable forest helps to stop deforestation. Buying **recycled** paper also helps save trees. Putting waste paper in recycling bins also helps.

▲ Forest fires can spread very quickly. They can also be very hard to put out.

Lost lands

Soil is an important **natural resource**. Farmers use it to grow **crops**. In dry, hot places, people can easily damage soil and make it useless.

Farm animals can damage soil. They eat the grass and plants that hold the soil together. The soil dries up and turns to dust. Then wind and rain blow and wash it away. This is called **erosion**. This erosion removes the top layer of soil where crops grow.

erosion   when rock or soil is worn away

▼ *Many of the world's deserts are getting bigger because of soil erosion.*

23

Homes of the future

This is the kind of house you may see in the future. This house is designed to use **renewable resources**. Renewable resources will not run out. 'Green' buildings like this use fewer **natural resources** than other buildings. Natural resources are things that come from the ground that people use. These buildings also make less **pollution**. Look at the labels to find out how.

This is a wind turbine. It uses **energy** from the wind to make electricity.

This house uses **solar power**. Panels on the roof change sunlight into **electricity**.

25

Looking Ahead

The number of people on our planet is growing quickly. Hundreds of thousands of people are born each day. More things will be needed as the number of people in the world grows. People will drive more cars and use more **electricity**. We will take more fresh water from Earth and cut down more trees.

In the future, the world will be an even busier place. Will it be able to provide people with what they need? What happens in the future depends on what people do now.

The future will be bright if more people use **renewable resources** such as wind and sunlight to power their homes and cars. Scientists may also find new ways to help us use fewer **nonrenewable resources** such as **fossil fuels**.

We should all **recycle** more of our waste and do what we can to make less **pollution**. We can all do our part to make the future bright. What are you going to do?

▲ Recycling more waste
is one way to help
make the future bright.

Get the Facts

Here are some facts to get you thinking about the world's **natural resources** and the future.

Forest facts

People began to cut or burn down trees around 11,000 years ago. Since then, more than half of the world's trees have been cut or burned down. Much of this has happened in the last 300 years, as these charts show.

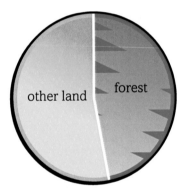

Forest cover in 1700

Forest cover in 2000

Recycling works!

It takes a lot of trees and water to make new paper. Making **recycled** paper helps to save trees. Making recycled paper also helps to save water.

Water use

This chart shows how much water is used in homes, farms, and factories around the world. Farming uses more water than homes and factories put together.

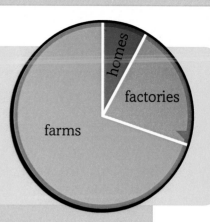

Saving water

A lot of water is wasted when **crops** are watered. The water washes into the soil before the plants can take it in. Some farmers use sprinklers that slowly drip water onto the crops to reduce this waste.

Fuel facts

In 2004 **nonrenewable resources** were used to make more than three-quarters of the world's **electricity** and fuel. Nonrenewable resources will run out one day.

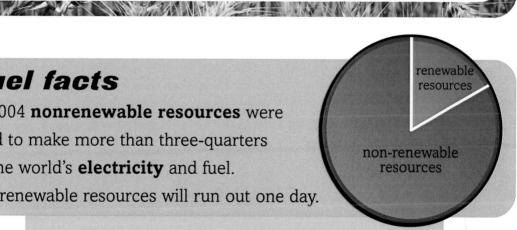

renewable resources

non-renewable resources

Fuel for the future

Solar power and wind power are being used to make electricity. The world could be getting almost half of its electricity from wind and solar power by 2020.

Glossary

crops plants that farmers grow to sell. Wheat, rice, and cotton are crops.

deforestation when trees in a forest are cut down. Some trees are burned to clear land. Other trees are cut down for the wood.

electricity source of power that makes machines work. Electricity runs computers and TVs.

erosion when rock or soil is worn away. Rivers, seas, wind, and rain can all cause erosion.

energy ability to make things move or change. Energy is needed to make electricity.

fertilizers chemicals that farmers put on crops to help them grow. Fertilizers make some plants grow more quickly.

fossil fuel material formed from the remains of plants and animals that died millions of years ago. Oil, gas, and coal are fossil fuels.

natural resources materials that people use that come from Earth, such as water. Other natural resources are soil, air, trees, and fossil fuels.

nonrenewable resources materials that people use that will run out one day. Oil is a nonrenewable resource. One day it will all be gone.

oil natural resource found under the ground that people use for fuel. Oil is also used to make plastic.

oxygen gas in the air that we need to breathe. Without oxygen, there would be no life on Earth.

pollution something that poisons or damages air, water, or land. Air pollution can be caused by smoke.

power station place that makes electricity. Many burn fossil fuels such as coal and gas to make electricity.

recycle change waste into something that can be used again. Paper, glass, plastics, and many other things can be recycled.

renewable resources resources that can be replaced. Sunlight, wind, and water are renewable resources.

sewage human waste carried away from people's toilets and drains. Most sewage is flushed down toilets.

solar power electricity made by using light or heat energy from the Sun. Some buildings use solar power to make all their electricity.

sustainable something that keeps going and does not run out. Trees are a sustainable resource if we plant new ones to replace those we cut down.

Want to Know More?

There is a lot to learn about the world's resources. These are some good places to look:

Books

- Ganeri, Anita. *Something Old, Something New: Recycling*. Chicago: Heinemann Library, 2005.

- Graham, Ian. *Fossil Fuels: A Resource our World Depends On*. Chicago: Heinemann Library, 2005.

- Greeley, August. *Poisoned Planet: Pollution in Our World*. New York: PowerKids Press, 2003.

Websites

- http://www.energyquest.ca.gov/

  Learn about renewable resources and find puzzles, information about scientists, and lots more. From the California Energy Commission.

- http://www.eia.doe.gov/kids/

  Visit this website to learn more about renewable and nonrenewable sources of energy. Play games and go on virtual field trips as well! Sponsored by the U.S. Department of Energy.

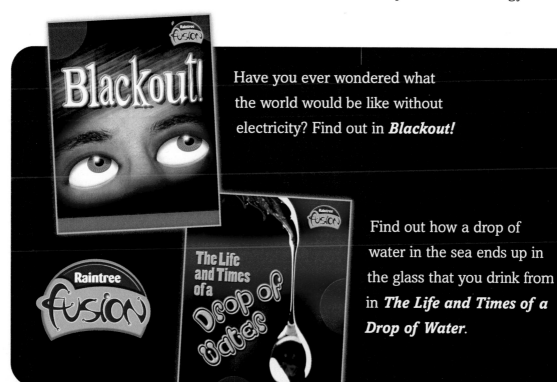

Have you ever wondered what the world would be like without electricity? Find out in *Blackout!*

Find out how a drop of water in the sea ends up in the glass that you drink from in *The Life and Times of a Drop of Water*.

Index